Why Don't You Drink Alcohol?

101Ways To Say I Quit Drinking Alcohol
Without It Being Awkward
(Sort Of)

By Sienna Green

To all the people who have asked me,
"Why Don't You Drink Alcohol?"
and made me feel awkward about it,
here's a little poem just for you:

Roses Are Red
Violets Are Blue
Alcohol Is Sh*t
And So Are You

Table of Contents

INTRODUCTION

There was a time in my life when suggesting I give up alcohol would have been like suggesting I give up breathing. Or eating. It wasn't something I even thought of as a choice. Drinking was an inevitable part of life, and my tendency to overdo it was also inevitable.

This isn't the case for everyone. Some people relate to alcohol in a 'healthy' way, in so much as imbibing poison can be healthy. Such people can apparently have one or two to 'take the edge off' or 'relax'. If you're anything like me, you regard these people as you would perhaps regard an unidentifiable alien life form that you had stumbled upon in the desert. Perhaps with a mix of fear, awe, reverence, and the feeling that you were witnessing something entirely beyond your comprehension.

Maybe you didn't pick up this book because you're like me. Perhaps you don't consider yourself an alcoholic, but you've thought about giving up booze for another reason. You may wish to support a partner, friend, or family member in their sobriety. You may have hit the age where the pain of the hangover starts to outweigh whatever enjoyment you got out of drinking the night before. You may just want to see if abstaining from alcohol improves your skin, waistline or bank balance (spoiler: it will). Even those who don't have a certifiable or apparent 'problem' with alcohol will benefit from going without it. The great thing about this adventure of becoming sober is there is no downside. Really, not a single one. You don't have to be anything like me to quit alcohol to change your life. So, breathe a sigh of relief. You don't have to have thrown up in your handbag because your hangover kicked in while you were wedged between two people in the backseat of your friend's car, stuck in morning traffic. You don't have to have been violently ill, hunched over the toilet bowl for hours while the boyfriend you blacked out and cheated on berates you from the doorway. You don't have to have taken a taxi to the emergency room shrieking uncontrollably because a hangover induced your first panic attack, and you thought you were dying. In other words, you don't have to be me. Quitting alcohol will still be good for you.

I've been sober for seven years now. I consider giving up booze the most important decision I've made in my life. As someone who has always struggled to stick to anything, I'm incredibly proud of my resolve. The only time I even think about drinking these days is when I'm watching one of the many reality shows I watch with my husband. As you're probably aware, the focal point of these shows is typically the drunken nights out. I watch, not longing to participate, but rather with an overwhelming sense of relief that I will never again experience another Morning After.

Never again will I groan awake in a too-bright room still wearing last night's clothes. Never again will I endure the headache that feels like my brain is trying to smash through my suddenly-shrunken skull. Never again will I experience the sense of impending doom that comes with the dawning, fragmented remembrances of the incriminating things I said or did. Or worse, the hours I have absolutely no recollection of at all.

The feeling of waking up fresh every morning never gets old.

What does get old though – is some f*ck wit asking me, "Why Don't You Drink Alcohol?" It really starts to mess with my zen after the tenth time of asking.

You start to understand why we live on such a drunk planet when alcohol is the only drug we have to justify NOT taking?!

It's still odd to me how f*cked up this whole question is. The fact that alcohol is a chemical depressant that releases the stress hormone cortisol (which makes us stressed!) and has the highest rating alongside radiation and asbestos for a substance linked to causing cancers - should be good enough reasons not to ask.

If anything, we should make them feel awkward by asking them, "Why Do You Drink Alcohol?"- it's literally one of the worst things you can do for every aspect of your life!

Yet we still have to justify not drinking. Not only that, but some people make you feel awkward about saying why you don't drink alcohol, as if we are some alien species. On the other hand, some might be intrigued and ask deeper questions, always wanting to discover if we had an exciting past (which couldn't be further from the truth by the end of my drinking career). Luckily the anonymous nature of my recovery means I only tell them so much or just make it up.

In telling people what they want to hear, I devised a game. A game where I could tell people whatever I wanted because why should I have to justify not drinking to anyone?

I shouldn't. So I had some fun with it.

Over the last seven years, I have lost count of the times people have asked me, "Why Don't You Drink Alcohol?" so much so that I decided to write a little book about it.

As you read the book – remember you have good c*nts and bad c*nts in life, and it's alright to swear. Australia is the best country in the world, and sharks kill very few people each year – Jaws got a bad rap.

But it's also worth remembering to OWN YOUR SOBRIETY. This book will uplift you to make your sobriety your own. Stop conforming to what society expects and start stepping into who you are mean't to be – and if it requires making up reasons why you don't drink alcohol – so be it.

Nothing is more powerful than wearing high heels, feeling sexy, sober and flirty – whilst holding a glass of tap water all night.

You do you – not them (unless they are hot, then do them lots – sober, of course ;)

Before we get onto the 101 ways to say "I Don't Drink Alcohol", firstly, a standard sober overshare about my life. Which, ironically, is another excellent way to stop people from asking you why you no longer drink alcohol!

A LITTLE BACKSTORY

I never seemed to be able to stop at that slight buzz, that warm feeling of confidence, conviviality, and possibility that seemed to unfold with those first few drinks of the evening.

It's not like I WANTED to blow up my life every time I drank. I wanted to stay in that positive headspace! I wanted to stay there so much that I just kept drinking. I'd drink way, way too quickly. I'd order rounds of shots and chug any liquid that appeared in front of me, desperate to keep the good feelings rolling. And then, in the blink of an eye, I'd be in the corner, openly weeping over a guy who turned me down while his housemate consoled me (he may or may not have also walked me home that night and tucked me into bed). Or I'd be climbing into my boss' lap. Or letting that guy I'd turned down several times tongue my ear. Why couldn't I ever stop when it was time to stop? Why couldn't I just stay in that headspace where I felt like my funniest, chattiest, and best self?

The simplest and most obvious explanation is sometimes the hardest to accept. Because I can't. I'm an alcoholic. I said these words for the first time several years ago, these words that are so plain as to seem trite. I said them, and something happened. I was freed. No more pressure to try and balance both drinking and not f*cking up my life. No more starting the night with a hopeless idea that I'd have a wholesome time and keep it under control. I am an alcoholic. There was no option but to cut the sh*t.

The Mayo Clinic defines alcoholism as 'a pattern of alcohol use that involves problems controlling your drinking, being preoccupied with alcohol, or continuing to use alcohol even when it causes problems.' It identifies binge drinking as a pattern where a male has five or more drinks within two hours or a female has at least four glasses within two hours. (Alcohol use disorder - Symptoms and causes - Mayo Clinic. https://www.mayoclinic.org/diseases-

conditions/alcohol-use-disorder/symptoms-causes/syc-
20369243)

I'm sure I'm not alone in being floored by this definition. In my twenties, I would have easily started a night out with four drinks within two hours. I would have started a night out MORE often with four drinks within about forty-five minutes. Many of you will undoubtedly be familiar with this type of 'pre-game'. The aim is to get as sh*t-faced as possible before you get to the club, bar, or party to avoid spending money on overpriced drinks. It wasn't uncommon for me to hit the town with a negative bank balance and no earthly idea how I would get home at the end of the evening, except some half-baked sense that I would somehow 'figure it out.' This went as well as you'd think it would most of the time. Since my standards when I was drunk dropped to the level of 'any man who was remotely interested in me and even some who treated me with active disdain,' I could always find a place to pass out.

One night that stands out amongst the vague memories of my twenties, I went out totally broke and met some friends at a pub. I managed to get suitably p*ssed, thanks to the generosity of the pals who had accepted as part of knowing me that I was perpetually skint. After my sloppy attempt at a kiss was rejected by a guy I'd previously hooked up with, I found myself outside the bar, alone, knowing I had no money for a taxi. A security guard looked at me with some concern and said, "You have a way of getting home, right?"

"Yeah," I think I groaned and proceeded to, I sh*t you not, lurch out into the night with the apparent intention of walking from Surry Hills to the flat I was staying at in Bondi Beach, stumbling drunk and wildly underdressed. I had been walking for about five minutes when, like a scene from a movie, it began to rain. Slopping along, I slipped and fell onto my arse on the sidewalk, where I started to bawl, wet, cold, and humiliated to the core of my being. I don't know how long I was on the ground, crying and soaking.

To this day, I can't believe what happened next. Of all the unmentionable and terrifying things that could have taken place while I was in that state, I was lifted to my feet by an unknown man who walked me to the nearest petrol station, withdrew fifty dollars from the ATM, flagged down a taxi, somehow managed to ascertain where I lived through my hysterics and sent me home. A man whose face and voice I remember nothing of, as unknowable to me as the night that I had wandered into. I remember only the shape of the events, nothing of the details. I couldn't tell you his appearance or how old he was. I'll never get to properly thank him for his care for a stranger, his utter lack of expectation of anything in return. Many women who find themselves vulnerable and defenceless while under the influence aren't as lucky as I was that night. We've seen their names and stories in the newspapers and on the evening shows. If you're anything like me, drinking made you push this type of luck over and over.

When I woke up the day after this incident, collecting my mental fragments, I resolved never to drink again. Somebody was looking out for me last night, I thought. This is a sign from the Universe, my guardian angels, whoever is paying attention, that it's time to make a change.

Just kidding. It took me another six years of making some of the worst f*cking decisions you've ever heard of to finally decide to 'maybe take a month off.' Alcohol is a hell of a drug. It was as though nothing could shake me awake. As part of my illness, I had simply accepted 'getting f*cked up' as inevitable. "I'm a f*ck-up, and I get f*cked up" could have been my mantra. Looking back, I realize how often I referred to myself as a 'loser'. It was nothing for me to talk horribly of myself. I was fully immersed in my misery, in what I thought was the inevitable and natural cycle of chasing that fleeting good feeling I'd have at the start of the night. But after a few drinks (literally just two!) I would go too far, do something incriminating or humiliating, feel like sh*t about myself, and then chase that fleeting, illusory good feeling again.

I had plans for my life beyond drinking. I'd studied theatre at Uni, and although it was during that course that I cemented my habit, I somehow managed to graduate and move to the city to pursue acting. I even found an agent, but mostly what I cared about when I got off work (at whatever day job I was tenuously holding on to) was going out. If I was meeting the girls from the clothing store I worked at, we'd gather at Suzy's house and down as many sickly sweet pre-mixed vodka drinks as we could before heading out to our favorite bar in Bondi Beach. If I was meeting friends from Uni or going out with one of my fellow underemployed actors, we'd usually work through a bottle or two of the cheapest wine we could get our broke hands on before wandering to a nearby pub. Somewhere in a typical night, I'd ditch my friends for some ill-advised hook-up and wake up in an unknown bed or a known but highly inappropriate bed, vaguely aware that I was supposed to be at work an hour ago. I'd rush home to change and eventually scurry into my job, always with an armful of liquids (you know, those mornings when you need a large coffee, a litre of water, and a gigantic smoothie as though this will somehow restore you to health). That was if I was having one of those mornings when I could tolerate ingesting anything at all. If it wasn't one of those, I'd spend the day having to pass my customers off while I dashed to the bathroom to heave up my stomach lining.

Since I was either being fired or skating on thin ice with my jobs and was always struggling to make my rent, I had very little bandwidth left to pursue what I claimed were my dreams. I fumbled through any auditions I managed to get, sometimes having just had several shots to 'calm my nerves', which were constantly frayed from a lack of preparation and a general sense that I was a 'f*ck-up' imposter and that everybody could see right through me. Needless to say, I never made it to Ramsey Street.

The Mayo Clinic's signs and symptoms of alcohol use disorder are as follows:

- Being unable to limit the amount of alcohol you drink

- Spending a lot of time recovering from alcohol use

- Feeling an intense craving or urge to drink alcohol

- Failing to fulfil significant obligations at work, school, or home due to repeated alcohol use

- Continuing to drink alcohol even though you know it's causing physical, social, work, or relationship problems

- Giving up or reducing social and work activities and hobbies to use alcohol

- Developing a tolerance to alcohol, so you need more to feel its effect, or you have a reduced impact from the same amount

Again, these are mostly all things that my younger self would have taken to be inevitable aspects of drinking alcohol rather than signs of a problem. There was no question of me having a problem. It was as though it wasn't even an option to NOT have a problem. I needed to drink fast, hard, and far too much to forget how much I hated myself enough to be around people.

My drinking had started relatively late for an Australian. I was at the legal age of 18 when I had my first, and the heavy drinking only began at university. My mum had never touched a drop, seeing how it ravaged her older brother's relationships, job prospects, and health. One of her preferred ways to self-medicate the mental after-effects of her dysfunctional childhood was to wage an unrelenting campaign of terror on everybody around her. This sounds like a harsh way to talk about one's mother. But for most of my life, she was verbally, physically and psychologically abusive towards my brother and me. Being all we knew, we didn't realize then that what was taking place was abuse, and we also didn't understand yet that it wasn't our fault.

We thought it was normal to incur hours of wrath, fury and insults over every tiny mistake or childish slip of the tongue we made. I really thought everyone's mother frequently leveraged cruel insults at them, and what's more, I thought she was entirely justified in doing so. I had no conception that I was dealing with someone who wasn't a reliable narrator. She was my mother, and I internalized everything she told me; I was stupid, useless, worthless, pathetic, fat, a moron, and a waste of space. I didn't have the awareness yet to understand that she was telling me all the things she secretly believed about herself.

It makes sense that when I started drinking, I started hard and fast. I wasn't doing it to 'take the edge off'. I had grown up believing I was utterly defective and unlovable. Why else would I be derided constantly by the one person who was supposed to love me unconditionally? The initial 'buzz' of the first few drinks was the only time I experienced anything resembling confidence. But what goes up must come down, and the black hole that enveloped me when I went past that buzz and entered 'f*ck it all' land contained all those years of buried trauma. After the high wore off, my feelings of worthlessness became all-consuming and sometimes dangerous.

Only later in life did I realize my mother's raging towards my brother and me was her attempt at coping with the voice in her head that told her she wasn't good enough. Unlike our father and the boyfriends she had after him, we couldn't talk back to her, or leave her. There was nothing we could do but silently absorb her insults and try to fortify ourselves against her episodes of rage by being as 'good' and unobtrusive as possible.

I didn't drink while I lived at home with her. If I was already in trouble just for existing, I wasn't about to push it. Instead of rebelling and partying, I withdrew socially. I found it challenging to make friends and was a constant target for bullies. Teenagers have a knack for sniffing out vulnerability. I was never invited to the type of parties where drinking was involved, which, I can see now, was much more of a blessing than I realized.

Then I turned 18, moved out of home and into a house with four other students from the theatre program I'd been accepted into, and in the tradition of repressed teenagers, went hog-f*cking-wild.

I can't remember, specifically, the first drink of my life. I can remember the experience of the first FEW drinks of any given night. The world opened up to me. Something surged through me akin to a desire to connect, to be close to my fellow human beings instead of recoiling from them in terror. It felt wonderful to feel comfortable socializing, able to participate in conversations without feeling as though everyone in the vicinity was giving me the side-eye, smirking at each other about my lameness, gathering the data and snippets of my attempts to chime in and connect, preparing to burst into laughter at my expense the moment I left the room. I became a part of life with those first few drinks, and I never wanted it to stop.

Of course, it always would. As anybody who can't stop at one, two, or three knows, that feeling can disappear as rapidly as it came on. When you are drinking to obliterate your self-consciousness, as I was, sometimes you end up destroying much more. It's one of the cruel jokes of drinking that those of us who partake in it to feel less socially awkward and more confident around others often end up destroying the very friendships, relationships, and connections we wanted so badly.

The faux-confidence alcohol bestows upon you, the feeling of benevolence and camaraderie with your fellow man, the lightness, the possibilities of the evening sprawling out before you; these are false friends (much like many of your drinking buddies).

Unlike the true confidence and self-assurance that comes from working on yourself, the false self-assurance you get from the alcoholic buzz can disappear as quickly and dramatically as it came on. All those feelings are illusory. True confidence and self-assurance around unfamiliar people and in uncomfortable social situations- can only come from knowing and-stay with me here- actually liking yourself. Alcohol leads you to do things that make you dislike yourself. Things you may regret for days, weeks, months, or even years. Things that make you have to apologize to people you never intended to hurt.

The advertising and media messages that help shape our society would have us think that a drug that can destroy our physical and mental health, financially ruin us, and cause us to do things that could land us in a hospital, prison, or the morgue is a desirable, even necessary product. The idea that alcohol is the elixir of good times, relaxation, and friendship is one of the most insidious marketing cons of all time.

Many people never question these ideas. The alcohol industry predominantly targets young audiences with the message that drinking is essential to celebration, fun, and bonding. We see this in every commercial featuring a group of friends celebrating their team's victory with a rousing cheer and a chug of beer and in every movie and TV show that shows the pinnacle of high school and university life as a raging party with flowing liquor.

Celebrity endorsements have always been a powerful tool, but what was once the domain of TV commercials is now even more insidious. Reality TV stars start their own wine companies, a convenient complement to the glamorous depiction of casual drinking their shows promote. Young influencers and models buzz about their investments in tequila brands, posting photos of them holding bottles next to their dewy, lovely faces as though the liquor is an indispensable part of their beauty routine.

The marketing would have you believe that alcohol makes you sexy, vibrant, and comfortable in your skin. Images explicitly targeted at women show elegant and perfectly-quaffed models, heads thrown back, eyes sparkling, surrounded by floating bubbles. It's pleasing, it's appealing, and it's safe. But alcohol companies are attempting to sell you qualities that are already within you. Charisma comes from feeling comfortable in your own skin. We've all seen those people who may not be the best dressed in the room or the best looking, but who nonetheless possess a certain magnetism. Their comfort with themselves makes people want to be around them. You don't know where they got it, but you know you want it.

But here's the rub. No one and nothing can give you that confidence. It comes from having accepted yourself on every level. And true self-acceptance becomes much harder to achieve when you hide your light behind a bottle of booze. You cannot gain that authentic, radiant inner confidence if you haven't faced your sh*t.

If you think you need alcohol to be 'yourself,' I'm here to tell you, from my experience, that you will become more 'yourself' by being sober than you can imagine. You will gain mental clarity and a sense of inner calm that you had previously thought impossible, and it will be all your own. It will not disappear with the light of dawn, with the drunkenness wearing off and the hangover death grip taking hold. It will not rapidly diminish as you piece together last night's events, realize the mortifying things you said or did, or frantically text friends asking, "I wasn't that bad, was I?"

Getting sober forced me to look at everything I had been trying to drown out. To finally understand that the abuse of my childhood had eroded any sense of self-worth I had and that there was no quick solution, no cheat code to instant confidence. There was nothing to do but attempt to give myself the unconditional love and support I'd never had.

Waking up safe in your own bed, remembering every part of the evening, knowing you were in complete control of your actions, having enjoyed yourself with friends, colleagues or partners without draining your bank account: nothing compares to this feeling. It is, somewhat paradoxically, incredibly freeing to be in control.

My decision to quit drinking for good occurred more with a whimper than a bang (despite all the misguided bangs of my twenties). I thought I'd take a month off. The resolve to take a month off became three months. By that stage, I was so proud, so encouraged by my ability to see something through, as someone who struggled to finish anything, that I eventually decided the decision would be for life. There was social anxiety and self-doubt at the beginning. Still, years later, I am stronger in my resolve than ever. I'm so enamored with the feeling of being in control of myself and my actions that I sometimes have bad dreams about slipping up, accidentally taking a drink, and not being able to recall what I said or did. Something I thought would be part of my life forever is actual nightmare fuel to me now.

If you're new to sobriety and not convinced you will actually enjoy it, imagine this; You're in a bar, maybe for a friend's birthday or another occasion you didn't want to miss out on, but you're lucid. You're steady on your feet. With perfect clarity, you survey the scene around you. A queue seemingly miles-deep at the bar, of people jostling and becoming frustrated amid their desire to part with their hard-earned cash. Regulars slumped on the stools, staring into the TV, their drinks, the abyss, barely noticing the commotion at their backs. And right in front of you, a person who's been blathering for twenty minutes about themselves and hasn't asked you a single question. And they're way too close, the alcohol pungent on their breath, spitwads flying out of their mouth and landing on your shoulder, which they don't even notice you trying to wipe away. And you realize that everyone in this place who is talking too loud and too close to a stranger THINKS they're making a genuine human connection. But how can it be when they don't remember it in the morning? When the person they thought they'd laid their soul bare to winds up saved in their phone as 'Shots Moustache'?

Alcohol precludes real human connection. That person you thought you were 'vibing' with might have simply been nodding along and humouring you because they didn't know how to say, "Excuse me, I have to leave." Or because they'd lost their friends and didn't want to be seen standing alone in front of the person they *really* liked. A drunk person is incapable of accurately perceiving the reality of a situation. Those seemingly positive social connections are based on falsehoods.

How often have you seen a group of people start the evening as the best of friends and end the night in an all-out brawl? Which of these options is indicative of the true nature of their relationship? What is real when alcohol is involved? They say, 'drunken words are sober thoughts.' Still, how often have we said things we regret when we've had too many? I know there was almost inevitably a point in the evening when my inebriated mind clicked over to the dark side. I was suddenly capable of saying cruel and untrue things I would have never uttered while sober.

Why take a chance? You can learn to be confident enough to be yourself without risking mouthing off in a way that will cause you and others pain. The personal power you will gain from navigating difficult social situations with a clear head is unparalleled. It will show the false, intoxicated confidence as the sham it is.

Having the courage to be free of liquid assistance will deepen and strengthen your relationships. It will attract the type of person you want in your life. You have everything you need within you. You just need to stop drowning it out.

Socializing is hard on the newly sober and the long-term sober alike. People may question your sobriety. They may not take you seriously. They may pressure you, continue to ply you with drinks and try to encourage others to ply you with drinks.

Those who buck up against the idea of you not drinking may not be consciously aware of why it rubs them the wrong way. Perhaps they feel that the sober version of you will see right through them and not think them as charming or hilarious as their inebriated buddies do. They may realize that when someone is sober, they have to work harder to impress them. Whatever it is, it's their problem, and while we know that it's perfectly fine to say "No, thanks," there's no harm in having a few retorts in your back pocket.

Meeting the question of why you're not drinking with humour enables you to show your personality. Laughter levels the playing field. If someone feels insecure in the presence of a sober person (and again, that is first and foremost their problem), you making light of the situation will help set them at ease.

As a disclaimer, I do not intend to pass judgment on those who partake or foster a culture of judgment. We're all on our own path. This guide aims to entertain and encourage you to stay the course of being sober. Most of the 101 ways I've come up with to say "I don't drink alcohol" are very silly; some are serious, and some may bring the conversation to a screeching halt. Use or don't use as you wish. Have fun. You've been warned.

HUMOROUS WAYS TO SAY "I DON'T DRINK ALCOHOL"

1. No thanks. I'm trying an experiment to see if people like me when I keep my top on.

2. I am f*cking insane without it.
(If you want to add fuel to the fire, it's on you chump)

3. I don't drink. If I wanted to wake up broke, shivering, and regretful, I'd buy more Crypto.
(I really thought I was on to something.)

4. The last time I drank, I woke up in a strange bathtub with stitches down my side. I'm not letting it happen a third time.
(On the flip side, they'll be really disappointed when your liver has no resale value!)

5. I can't stand the bar scene. If I want to watch rambling idiots run into things, I hang out with my kids.

(We know you really love your kids *wink *)

6. I'm sober these days, although sometimes I'll kick a stranger in the face over a stolen bar stool just for old-time's sake.

(I haven't done it, but I've witnessed it.)

7. I don't drink alcohol because I'm training for the 2068 Olympics.

(That should get them thinking.)

8. I don't drink anymore, but sometimes I still piss all over the floor and eat three large pizzas to relax.

9. I wanted to become insufferable about something, so I chose sobriety. Can I tell you how amazing I feel?

(The overshare is my absolute fave)

10. I don't drink anymore. Even the GOAT has to retire sometime.

(Try this one on your American friends!)

11. I can't, I already have a lifetime ban from this place. Sh*t, they've seen me.
(And then you duck and run. Foolproof.)

12. I don't need to drink. I already wake up with a sense of impending doom. Did you hear about the asteroid on a collision course with Earth?

13. I hate how booze makes people start close-talking. Breath mint?

14. My daddy said I'm not allowed to spend my allowance on booze anymore.
(What kind of daddy? They won't know! And more importantly, they'll be too disturbed to ask.)

15. I would have a drink, but my self-driving car has really been doing its own thing lately.

16. This isn't a watch – its my alcohol sensor given to me by the judge. Beep beep beep.
(Good to use if you need to get out of a convo)

17. I quit drinking. I wanted to lose weight without giving up my morning pizza.

(It never ceases to amaze me the wackadoodle things people will try to shed some pounds instead of just...cutting back on alcohol.)

18. I quit drinking to catch up on all the books I was too p*ssed to read at Uni.

(The other day, I declared to my husband, 'Wow, Dostoyevsky was really good,' as though I were making some sort of discovery.)

19. I got sober so I could focus on my recording career. I'm learning to play the recorder.

(Do yourself a favor and search 'See You Again recorder cover' on Youtube.)

20. When you have a template for a morning-after apology ready to go on your phone, it's time to give it a rest.

21. No thanks. I don't want to get drunk and sleep with somebody really hot.

(So embarrassing!)

22. I gave up the booze when I decided to convert my wine cellar into a sex dungeon.
(Be prepared for questions.)

23. No thanks; I want to be able to leave without making a scene.
(It is MUCH easier to do the Irish Goodbye when you're not stumbling to the door, smashing into tables, and breaking glasses.)

24. I wish I could have a drink, but I'm Batman.

25. I don't drink anything I don't know how to spell, and, between you and me, I'm illiterate.

26. I only drink at Wham! shows.
(Insert any other now-defunct band you can think of.)

27. It's the 20's. Haven't you heard of prohibition?
(Boom-tsh!)

28. No thanks, I can't go viral again.
(There's no such thing as 'Dance like nobody's watching.' Everybody's watching, they have their

phones out, and you're about to become a TikTok meme.)

29. Oh no, I'm capable of making stupid decisions on my own. Wanna see a photo of my kids?
(Again, we know you really love your kids.)

30. Not tonight; I have to be up at dawn to feed the hog.
(Nobody needs to know who 'the hog' is.)

31. Alcohol is a depressant, and I've already watched the news today.

32. Alcohol kills brain cells, and I'm losing enough in this conversation.
(Roasted.)

33. I'm allergic to alcohol. It makes me break out in The Robot.
(Hi, Dad!)

34. I like to be able to blackmail my friends with the sh*t they do when they're drinking.
(Just like they have all done to me!)

35. I'm in AA. I'm not addicted to alcohol, just terrible coffee.

(But seriously, complimentary coffee is always welcome, and I'll eat those weird little biscuits even if nobody else does.)

36. I don't drink. My dad was a raging alcoholic and I don't want to make him proud.

(A bit of a mood-killer if you're into that sort of thing.)

37. I knew it was time to quit when I saw that **BBC** News story on alcohol intolerance. They used a bunch of my Facebook photos.

(Aggressively purging any trace of your past from Facebook should be one of the Twelve Steps.)

38. I only drink Vulcan Ale. Live long and prosper!

(Bonus points for adding the Vulcan Salute. Extra bonus points for doing it incorrectly.)

39. No thanks, I'm on an Ayahuasca Journey tonight.

(Bonus points for saying this while being obviously stone-cold sober.)

40. I came here to chew bubblegum and judge people who drink, and I'm all out of bubblegum.
(If they don't get the reference, they'll be too confused to keep bothering you anyway.)

41. Yeah, casually drinking poison and just hoping I don't die is kinda weird to me. But you do you!
(Your body sees alcohol as poison. The liver's job is to help your body break it down and eliminate it using an enzyme called alcohol dehydrogenase. Your organs want the sh*t out of your body. Your organs!)

42. Whenever I drink, I hear 'All Along The Watchtower' in my head and put my fist through a wall.
(Doesn't it just get you amped up?)

43. I had to quit. I used to wake up just so sick of winning karaoke competitions.
(Plus, everyone was sick of me singing "Wannabe" by the Spice Girls every time.)

44. I knew I had a problem when I made my local takeaway pizza my emergency contact. And then I called them when I fell down the stairs.

45. I've invented too many dance moves, and I'm sick of not getting any credit.

46. My friends tell me whenever I have too many, I start yelling about the moon landing being fake. *(Insert any conspiracy theory you think might put someone off here. Even if it's true.)*

47. The last time I drank, I mistook my roommate's haemorrhoid cream for my toothpaste. And then I f*cked him. *(Classic mix-up!)*

48. My downstairs neighbours were sick of me getting drunk and trying to teach myself kickflips.

49. Whenever I drink, I p*ss myself, and I'm not wearing my rubber pants tonight.

50. I don't drink anymore, but if I feel tempted, I'll just tell you the same story three times in a row and punch myself in the face.

51. I'm not cute enough to get out of being arrested anymore.

(Shoutout to the police officer who kindly let me off the hook when that irate cab driver I couldn't pay flipped out and drove me straight to the station.)

52. I'm practising a form of meditation where I just let the horrors of the world wash over me and don't try to numb them out.

(Mindfulness!)

53. I want to set an example for my kids by actually putting coffee in my coffee cup.

(It's like you're one of those 'Mummy wine time' memes come to life!)

54. I'm staying sober so I'm in a better position to help others. Your fly's undone.

(You'd be better off just zipping it.)

55. I converted to Mormonism. Let me tell you more.......

(Bonus points if you pull out the bible)

56. I quit drinking so I could live longer and see how the f*ck this all ends.

(I mean, don't you want to live forever just to see what happens?)

57. Oh, I'm already drunk with power.

58. I don't need to drink to become the worst version of myself.

(I just have to get stuck in traffic in peak hour.)

59. I'm a flaneur; I need my powers of observation.

(Just showing off a word I learned in my sobriety.)

60. I only wanna set the dance floor on fire metaphorically from now on.

61. Hangovers are a waste of time; there are only 80 hours a week, and I need them to improve my math skills.

62. I loved drinking, but now that I'm trying 'not to ruin my life', I'm realizing I like that too.

63. I only allow myself one vice at a time, and I'm not gonna stop buying rare Beanie Babies.

64. I knew it was time to quit drinking and hooking up when I scored 100% on my STD test.

FLIRTY WAYS TO SAY
"I DON'T DRINK ALCOHOL"

65. We could have so many years of erectile dysfunction ahead of us. Why speed up the process?

66. I'm much wittier when I'm sober, and I want to impress you with my ability to remember your name. What is it again? (*wink)

67. I don't need a drink; I like the vibe just as it is.

68. Ubers are expensive, and one of us will have to drive us back to your place.
(Awooga!)

69. I already feel woozy in your presence.

70. I don't want to be stuck waiting at the bar when I could be talking to you.

WAYS TO SAY
"I DON'T DRINK ALCOHOL"
THAT WILL STOP THEM
ASKING AGAIN!

71. I'm pregnant/trying to conceive.

(Most medical professionals advise against drinking, even in moderation, while you're trying to become pregnant. And, of course, alcohol use at any level during pregnancy is known to contribute to instances of miscarriage, stillbirth, and a range of lifelong physical, behavioral, and intellectual disabilities.)

72. I know myself, and I know I can't hold my alcohol.

(Sincere, uncomplicated, and disarmingly honest. No one can argue with the idea that you don't want to embarrass yourself or put yourself in a dangerous situation.)

73. I'm allergic – alcohol makes me feel ill.
(Much like saying you have explosive diarrhoea, no one in their right mind will argue with a person who says, 'I don't want to get sick.')

74. I don't like to support the alcohol industry.
(And with good reason. Excessive alcohol use is responsible for thousands upon thousands of deaths, injuries, and illnesses worldwide each year. In the United States alone, the numbers are staggering: excessive alcohol use led to more than 140,000 deaths and 3.6 million years of potential life lost (YPLL) each year in the United States from 2015 – 2019, shortening the lives of those who died by an average of 26 years. (https://www.cdc.gov/alcohol/fact-sheets/alcohol-use.htm) And yet, alcohol is aggressively marketed as the essence of good times and even an essential part of life.)

75. Alcohol doesn't align with my values/religion/spirituality.
(Whether this is true for you or not, few people will argue with you about your religious or spiritual beliefs

*in a social situation. And if they do, you have the
perfect excuse to walk away and not engage with them
further. Or ask them to come with you to a 'meeting'
to find out why you don't drink anymore – they will
either run away or might actually need the support!)*

76. Alcohol interacts with my medication.
*(As mentioned above, your medical history and what
medication you may take are private matters, and most
reasonable people will understand this. If you want to
stop them from going down the rabbit hole any further
– just say you are on anti-biotics for aggressive vaginal
blisters.)*

77. I don't drink alcohol for health reasons.
*(Your health reasons could be that alcohol causes a
significantly increased risk of high blood pressure,
heart disease, stroke, liver disease, various cancers,
dementia, mental health issues, and dependency.
Enough?)*

78. I have alcoholism in my family and don't want to risk it.

(Medical researchers have identified eleven genes associated with the risk of excessive drinking and compulsive behaviours around alcohol (alcohol.org).)

79. I'm driving tonight.

(Taxis and rideshares are expensive, the trains don't always run this late at night, and you're a responsible adult who doesn't flagrantly put the lives and limbs of yourself and others at risk through drunk driving. Solid.)

80. I don't have any tolerance for alcohol anymore.

(Most people over 30 will understand this one pretty implicitly. There's a certain point when we realize we can't drink as we used to. I like to think of it as nature's way of reminding us that we're not invincible and getting us off the booze before it can start to wreak havoc on our bodies, minds, and lives.)

81. I've had too many bad experiences with alcohol in the past.

(Sadly, almost everyone has. Being upfront about it may open you up to an uncomfortable conversation, but showing vulnerability can also invite greater connection and understanding.)

82. I like to be able to look out for my friends.

(Always a good reminder when it comes to your sobriety – the friends that mind, don't matter, and the ones that don't mind, matter.)

83. My partner/spouse doesn't drink.

(Doubles as a way to tell someone that you're spoken for!)

84. My kids don't like it when I drink.

(They get weirded out when Mummy does The Worm.)

85. My dog doesn't like it when I drink.

(He also gets weirded out when Mummy does The Worm.)

86. I have work to do when I get home tonight.
(Whether it's your memoir, your kid's homework, or the dishes, you need your sh*t together.)

87. I actually have more fun without it.
(This may not feel true initially, but it will eventually.)

88. I feel safer when I'm sober.
(It's crazy to think how many dangerous situations alcohol has put me in over the years. You never get bored of being in control – until the kids return from school!)

89. I had my drink spiked, and ever since then, I've stuck to bottled water.
(A shocking 1 in 9 women in the UK say they've had their drink spiked, with 4 in 10 women saying they believe they would not be taken seriously if they reported it.
(https://www.independent.co.uk/news/uk/home-news/drink-spiking-women-police-b1956508.html) I always stick to bottled water if I have to be at a bar. It gives me something to do with my hands, and I don't have to worry.)

90. I really don't like how it makes me feel.

(*If someone gave you a pill that made you feel spaced out, say things you would regret, feel anxious for days after and make you vulnerable to preying men – would you take it? It's a complete sh*t show we have to justify not taking alcohol!*)

91. I can't control my swearing when I drink.

(*Are you a good c*nt or a bad c*nt? An Aussie favorite!*)

92. I'm trying to improve my marriage/relationship.
(Probably best to use this line with your close friends to avoid the impending awkwardness of opening up too much too soon to a stranger!)

93. I quit drinking to support a family member/partner, and it made me feel so good I kept it up.

94. I tried Dry January, which made me feel so amazing that I kept it up and now do Dry Day......
every day.

(ODAAT – *Sobriety really is the gift that keeps on giving.*)

95. Hangovers give me panic attacks.

(Hanganxiety describes the feeling of doom that can set in the morning after a big night due to sleep deprivation, dehydration, and the dawning realization of what you said or did. I personally ended up at the emergency room more times than I can count, convinced I was dying the day after a session. Sunday Funday!)

96. I only have one liver.

(*Googles quickly* Yeah, it's one of those organs we only have one of.)

97. I can't stand the taste of alcohol.

(I used to think I loved fruity cocktails, it turns out I just loved sugar.)

98. I don't drink alcohol for so many reasons. How long have you got?

(Watching the fear quickly appear on a drinker's face when they get stuck with the confident non-drinker who LOVES talking about sobriety never gets old – make them squirm!)

99. I don't drink alcohol; it puts me to sleep (badly!).
(*Alcohol is literally the worst thing you can do for consistent sleep – don't worry, another 101 book is impending on all of the worst things that alcohol does.*)

100. I don't drink alcohol; I'm a non-conformist.
(*Is it just me, or is the culture more conformist than ever? Remember when people rebelled against corporations and major brands having an outsized influence on our tastes and preferences? Be an iconoclast. Order a glass of tap water.*)

101. No, thanks. I don't drink.
(*Said with unwavering confidence and conviction, this could be the most potent line on this list. But inevitably, through years of experience, the drunk ones always keep asking why! We just act as a mirror for their own behaviors!*)

And remember the poem at the start of the book for those who make you feel awkward about your sobriety:

Roses are Red
Violets are Blue
Alcohol is Sh*t
And so are you.

Whatever you choose to say, your sobriety is your own. You should never be made to feel anything less than epic, just because you want a better life. So stay strong and sip that tap water like a boss.

CONCLUSION

Unfortunately, we live on a very drunk planet. Alcohol is so integrated into the fabric of our existence that many people go their entire lives never questioning why they choose to drink or thinking about the reasons someone would have for not partaking. One of the cruelest elements of society is that while alcohol is normalized as the key to sociability, friendship, and good times, people who routinely overindulge are vilified. This isn't to say that actions shouldn't have consequences. But the idea of making a hazardous drug like alcohol an integral part of the culture and then treating with contempt those who make poor choices or become addicted ought to be seriously scrutinized.

If someone you associate with is pressuring you to drink or is otherwise unsupportive of your sobriety, consider whether it may be time to take a step back from this person or downsize their influence in your life. Think about why someone who supposedly cares about you would want you to be in a position wherein you are vulnerable to making poor choices and messing with your mental, emotional, financial, and physical well-being.

More often than not, people are afraid to confront their own issues and will project their insecurity onto you. People will always tell on themselves. If they imply that people who don't drink are boring, it's because they feel they're boring without a drink. If they say you need to have one and 'loosen up,' it's because they need to loosen up. If they were so relaxed, they wouldn't care who drinks and who doesn't! People who consistently pressure you to imbibe don't care about anything but not being left alone in the pit they're digging for themselves. Again, this is not your responsibility.

The key to staying the course of sobriety and standing by your convictions is always to understand your 'Why?' Why are you choosing not to drink?

In conversation with Dua Lipa on her podcast At Your Service, sober sage Russell Brand said something that made me immediately hit pause and write it down: "The word Recovery means that we *recover* the person we were intended to be." Who were you intended to be? What does the life you ought to be living involve? What do you visualize yourself doing and achieving?

Maybe it's not about anything concrete or material; perhaps you simply wish to become more grounded and calm. I know that after I quit drinking, I stopped having panic attacks. I had never made the connection between the dehydration and physical depletion of a hangover and the heart palpitations, shakes, and anxiety that would overwhelm my body, causing me to enter into a tunnel of imminent doom. What do you hope to gain from not drinking (nay, what WILL you gain from not drinking?) What are you most looking forward to getting back? All those extra hours you wasted on hangovers? What would you like to do with your Sundays instead? Take a long hike in a national park you've always wanted to visit? Take up meditation and contemplate how clear and free your mind feels without the chattering anxiety of a hangover? Start making your way through the pile of novels that's been gathering dust on your nightstand for a year (might I recommend this guy Dostoyevsky)?

The possibilities are expansive beyond your imagination.

Being sober can feel like an isolating experience. If you're anything like me, you've felt profound envy for those who can have 'just one or two,' reap that initial feeling of relaxed confidence and call it a damn night. Acceptance that you may have a propensity for alcohol abuse is hard at first. You may feel that the situation is unfair, and you're right.

In addition to alcoholism, I've struggled with severe anxiety since I was around twelve. By that age, I had already been through several Adverse Childhood Experiences (commonly known as ACEs), which are traumatic childhood events deemed major contributing factors to depression, anxiety, drug dependency, and alcoholism in adulthood. The seed was planted in me at a very young age. I have learned to accept this and understand that it was not something I had conscious control over and wasn't my fault. From the time I first started drinking, alcohol was not something I could enjoy in moderation but something I poured down my throat as fast as possible to drown out all the mental noise, intrusive thoughts, and hurt of my upbringing. It was my medicine before I discovered actual medicine, which while not an option for everybody, has mercifully agreed with me and reduced my anxiety symptoms to a life-changing extent. I don't reprimand myself for not having better self-control anymore or wallow in shame about how inebriated I used to get. I practise self-forgiveness when I find myself heading down that rabbit hole. I was doing the best I could with the mind that I had.

Letting go of any shame you may feel that other people can drink within moderation and that you cannot is crucial. There is nothing wrong with knowing and respecting your limitations. Take pride in the fact that you have acquired this inner knowledge.

Whether you're new to abstaining from alcohol or have been sober for a while, I hope this book has given you some guidance, affirmation, and hopefully a few laughs (I certainly tried). Although being the only one not drinking alcohol at a social occasion can feel very exposing at first, you are far from alone. When you take your power back by choosing to say no, you open yourself up to a new world of potential: of the person you could become, the experiences you could have, and the people you could meet. False friends will drop away, and the connections you make sober will be more profound and meaningful than you could have imagined because they're based in reality. More importantly, you'll get to know yourself, and it will feel as though the possibilities of your life are expanding before you. Those dreams you've been cradling in the back of your mind because you needed to focus on just getting through another day with a hangover? You might suddenly find yourself with the time and mental energy to pursue them. Or your ideas about who you thought you were may drastically change.

After I quit drinking, I realized that I had held a dream of being an actor all those years for entirely the wrong reasons. I didn't really love the art of performance; I just wanted fame and adulation so I could finally feel like I was *enough*. When I became sober, I was forced to face my lack of self-worth and begin building my self-esteem from scratch. My wish for my life now is to be one of service, not celebrity. Through writing, I want to help other people stop running from the truth of who they really are and inspire them to heal what they were trying to numb with alcohol.

You've lost enough time to hangovers, apology texts, working a job you despise and contemplating your regrets. Don't be afraid to be who you were always intended to be.

If you have enjoyed this short read (even with the obligatory sober overshare at the beginning), I would be grateful if you could leave a short review on Amazon, even if it's a few sentences long (check the next page for more details on how).

Thanks for reading.

LEAVE A REVIEW

If you have enjoyed reading "Why Don't You Drink Alcohol?" - It would be amazing if you could leave a short review on Amazon, even if it's just a few sentences long.

It really does help keep the sparkling water flowing.

Please scan below, according to where you are from, to leave a review on Amazon:

United Kingdom

United States

Australia

Canada

Rest of the World

Thank you!

EXCITING OPPORTUNITY –
EARLY REVIEW TEAM

Would you like to be part of the early review team for future book releases? Get your hands on the early review copies and most importantly, you get to see epic books before they get released.

MORE BOOKS BY THE PUBLISHER:

THE INTERNATIONAL BESTSELLER

THE INTERNATIONAL BESTSELLER

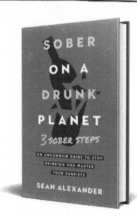

SCAN ME

NEED EXTRA SUPPORT
IN SOBRIETY?

If you need extra support in life – you can join the Sober On A Drunk Planet Community – they're a good bunch of c*nts on a similar path and slaying life sober.

Made in the USA
Middletown, DE
30 March 2023